Be With Me, Lord

PRAYERS FOR THE SICK

Rodney J. DeMartini

017196

WLP

WORLD LIBRARY PUBLICATIONS
the music and liturgy division of J. S. Paluch Company, Inc.
3708 River Road, Suite 400 • Franklin Park, Illinois 60131-2158
800 566-6150 • www.wlpmusic.com

Be With Me, Lord

PRAYERS FOR THE SICK

WLP 017196

ISBN 978-1-58459-245-7

Author: Rodney J. DeMartini
Editor: Jerry Galipeau
Copy Editor: Marcia T. Lucey
Typesetting and Design: Denise C. Durand

Contents

Contents (continued)

Introduction

Now Simon's mother-in-law was in bed with a fever, and they told Jesus about her at once. He came and took her by the hand and lifted her up. Then the fever left her, and she began to serve them. *(Mark 1:30–31)*

This Gospel scene has special significance for both the sick person and the minister to the sick. Yet Mark's brief and non-detailed description leaves us with a question: "How can the healing touch of Jesus be personally experienced by the sick?"

Illness is a common occurrence in the life of every person just as it was for this un-named woman in the Gospel. It disrupts our living pattern; often produces feelings of self-pity, helplessness, and loneliness; and reminds us that physically we are fragile and mortal. Thus, whether we are pestered by a common cold, hospitalized for a routine operation, or faced with the tragic news of terminal cancer, we share a common need. It is a need to replace our fears and frustrations with a sense of confidence and courage. It is a need to experience personally the comfort and peace of being touched by the Lord.

The inevitability of illness certainly does not ensure that we can accept its effects willingly or even find effective ways to show our love and support for those whom we love who are sick. Too often the reactions of denial and discomfort turn us in upon ourselves to brood or worry aimlessly. The inherent power of our Christian faith to raise our fallen spirit is not called upon. Jesus could have simply visited his friend's mother-in-law and his very presence would have been a caring gesture. Yet he chose to intervene directly and powerfully. Jesus called upon his faith and hers to place this illness in the hands of a loving Father. The power of Jesus' outstretched hand enabled this woman to reach out and serve. This same power and care are the basic inspiration for the prayer forms in this book.

In turning to scripture as a basic component of these prayer units, I believe that we can encounter the most helpful recollections and insights of people who experienced, as we do, the human condition. We need to be reminded that despite our hurts and limitations, especially evident in illness, we have the irrevocable promise of God's personal love and the gift of being saved through the sufferings of Jesus. Our God is not any less familiar with pain and weakness than we are; God understands and even seeks to share the burden of our hurt and offers personal support.

I have turned to the psalms because of their sensitivity to the whole range of human emotions—anger and thanksgiving, anxiety and peace. Many of the psalms acknowledge the basic enemies of life and candidly remind God that our strength alone is not sufficient to conquer these forces. The psalms call upon God without covering over intense feelings. The psalmist is not afraid to shake his fist at God, knowing that the Lord is not turned away by the honest expressions of those created in God's image. God is not just a fair-weather friend.

Moreover, we should recall that it was the anguished cry of Psalm 22 that was placed on the lips of Jesus on the cross. Feeling helpless and alone in the hands of his enemies, Jesus speaks out his feelings of self-pity and hopelessness, realizing that only God could understand and care for him in this time of intense need.

It is appropriate to rely upon the expressive words of the psalmist. These cries of real human need can be a springboard of prayer for us. God, who is the source of life, will not turn a deaf ear to those in need.

The use of New Testament readings is based upon their value as foundation statements for the Christian life. The many characters and events speak to the human condition and to the persistent attempts of God to minister to all people. The passages were chosen to reiterate familiar incidents in the life of Jesus and the early church, focusing especially on the search for those realities that are permanent and life-giving. Illness so often makes us disrupted; thus we need to be reaffirmed in the timeless words of the scriptures. In addition, the scriptures can be an antidote to loneliness and self-absorption. We are reminded in these words that we are part of a larger Christian community extended throughout the ages. We can be led to a sense of commonality with people who, like us, are suffering, but who have turned to the scriptures for comfort and meaning.

The closing prayers are original compositions designed to summarize the scriptural themes. The language is direct, reiterating the personal conviction of the author that feelings of anger, loneliness, and frustration can be offered as prayer. Sick people do not need the additional burden of feeling guilty for their feelings or being forced to suppress their complaints to God. Yet every prayer ends with the Easter alleluia as a reminder that death and the forces of fear and weakness have been overcome once and for all in Jesus. God will not turn a deaf ear to our cries; we have been given that promise through the resurrection of Jesus, God's Son and our brother.

These prayers are primarily intended to be used by a person who is ill. At the same time, those who visit and minister to the sick can find in them an expression of their sentiments, which are sometimes too difficult to reveal. Through these expressions of common faith, the sick person and the visitor will extend the boundaries of their relationship, no matter how casual or intimate. Together, they can call out to a God who knows and loves the human condition and who continually redeems it. There is no better comfort we can give to one another than this reassurance.

I Am Afraid, Lord!

You can turn to the following prayers on those days when you feel especially afraid and powerless in the face of your illness. Your normal routine has been disrupted and you feel cut off from those you love. Your anger and frustration need to be spoken; it hurts too much to keep these feelings bottled up inside.

Place yourself—with all your feelings—in the care of your Father, letting God know how weary you feel. You want to be heard and you sense God's personal presence to you in your illness. Seek to understand how Jesus dealt with the disappointment of suffering in his own life and try to see this time as one in which you can grow in faith and trust. Let spiritual strength counter the weariness of your body.

Come Save Me, Lord

Jesus reminds us of the healing and uplifting power of faith.

Go and tell John what you hear and see: the blind receive their sight, the lame walk, the lepers are cleansed, the deaf hear, the dead are raised, and the poor have good news brought to them. And blessed is anyone who takes no offense at me.

(Matthew 11:4–6)

Psalm 6:1–9

Jesus, Healer of the Sick and Troubled

O LORD, do not rebuke me in your anger,
   or discipline me in your wrath.
Be gracious to me, O LORD,
      for I am languishing;
   O LORD, heal me, for my bones
      are shaking with terror.
My soul also is struck with terror,
   while you, O LORD—how long?

Turn, O LORD, save my life;
   deliver me for the sake
      of your steadfast love.
For in death there is no remembrance
      of you;
   in Sheol who can give you praise?

I am weary with my moaning;
   every night I flood my bed with tears;
   I drench my couch with my weeping.
My eyes waste away because of grief;
   they grow weak because of all my foes.

Depart from me, all you workers of evil,
   for the LORD has heard the sound
      of my weeping.
The LORD has heard my supplication;
   the LORD accepts my prayer.

Responsory

Jesus said, ". . . All things can be done for the one who believes."

"I believe; help my unbelief!"

(Mark 9:23, 24)

Prayer

Jesus, my Lord and brother, come quickly as the darkness of despair looms over me.

Help me not to lose heart or hope.

Send your life-giving Spirit to enable me to offer my sufferings faithfully in union with your saving passion and death on the cross.

May your name be blessed forever!

Amen. Alleluia!

Why Me, Lord?

*Those who followed Jesus knew of his
compassion for the sick.*

Now a certain man was ill, Lazarus of
Bethany, the village of Mary and her sister
Martha. So the sisters sent a message to
Jesus, "Lord, he whom you love is ill." But
when Jesus heard it, he said, "This illness
does not lead to death; rather it is for God's
glory, so that the Son of God may be
glorified through it."

(John 11:1, 3–4)

Psalm 13

The Lord will answer.

How long, O LORD? Will you forget me
    forever?
  How long will you hide your face
    from me?
How long must I bear pain in my soul,
  and have sorrow in my heart all day long?
How long shall my enemy be exalted
    over me?

Consider and answer me, O LORD my God!
  Give light to my eyes, or I will sleep
    the sleep of death,
and my enemy will say, "I have prevailed";
  my foes will rejoice because I am shaken.

But I trusted in your steadfast love;
  my heart shall rejoice in your salvation.
I will sing to the LORD,
    because he has dealt bountifully with me.

Responsory

I am the resurrection and the life. Those who believe in me, even though they die, will live.

(John 11:25)

Prayer

Lord, I am angry and confused; my sickness is beginning to overwhelm me.

I want to give so much more in life, O God; so many things I have left undone or unsaid.

I humbly ask that you give me the strength to accept my present illness and, if it be your will, that I might regain my health.

Forgive my impatience and my unbelief in your constant care for me.

I pray in union with Jesus your Son, who overcame suffering and death in his glorious resurrection.

Amen. Alleluia!

God Is My Shield

Jesus reminds his followers that suffering patiently borne leads to the joy of resurrection.

If any want to become my followers, let them deny themselves and take up their cross and follow me. For those who want to save their life will lose it, and those who lose their life for my sake will find it. For what will it profit them if they gain the whole world but forfeit their life? Or what will they give in return for their life?

(Matthew 16:24–26)

Psalm 7:1–2, 6, 10–11, 17

Jesus, my model in the face of despair

O LORD my God, in you I take refuge;
    save me from all my pursuers,
        and deliver me,
or like a lion thy will tear me apart;
    they will drag me away, with no one
        to rescue.

Rise up, O LORD, in your anger;
    lift yourself up against the fury
        of my enemies;
    awake, O my God;
        you have appointed a judgment.

God is my shield,
    who saves the upright in heart.
God is a righteous judge,
    and a God who has indignation every day.

I will give to the LORD the thanks
        due to his righteousness,
    and sing praise to the name of the LORD,
        the Most High.

Responsory

Oh, restore me to health and make me live!
You have held back my life from the pit of
destruction.

(Isaiah 38:16b, 17b)

Prayer

Lord Jesus, I feel weak and helpless
in my illness and I want to escape
and hide from the possibility of
death.

Once again, I am seeking false
comfort for the moment in the denial
of death, but I know that this can
only lead to anger and despair.

Rise up, Lord, and strengthen me
now in this time of trial; forgive me
for doubting that your grace is always
with me.

Give me patience with those who
seek to comfort me in my illness and
courage to face the future.

I make this prayer in union with you,
Lord Jesus, who accepted sufferings
more painful than mine.

Amen. Alleluia!

Be with Me, Lord

Jesus calls us to give example in our lives even when illness drains our strength.

You are the light of the world. A city built on a hill cannot be hid. No one after lighting a lamp puts it under the bushel basket, but on the lampstand, and it gives light to all in the house. In the same way, let your light shine before others, so that they may see your good works and give glory to your Father in heaven.

(Matthew 5:14–16)

Psalm 4:1–3, 7a, 8
Lord, I am afraid.

Answer me when I call, O God of my right!
　　You gave me room when I was in distress.
　　Be gracious to me, and hear my prayer.

How long, you people, shall my honor
　　　suffer shame?
　　How long will you love vain words,
　　　and seek after lies?

But know that the LORD has set apart
　　　the faithful for himself;
　　the LORD hears when I call to him.

You have put gladness in my heart.

I will both lie down and sleep in peace,
　　for you alone, O LORD,
　　　make me lie down in safety.

Responsory
"Blessed are those who mourn,
for they will be comforted."

(Matthew 5:4)

Prayer

Father, the reality of death touches
me personally in my present illness.

It is hard to remain at peace and
accept the fact that I may soon pass
from this life.

Yet I want to be a sign of hope to
others that death is not the end,
but an opportunity for more intimate
union with you.

Give me the strength of your grace
so that I may witness to this belief
more faithfully, and may I always give
you thanks and praise for the persons
and events that have entered my life.

I pray this in union with your Son
and my brother, Jesus, who did not
give in to fear or despair in his
suffering.

Amen. Alleluia!

I Trust in You, O God

The great apostle Saint Paul gives us assurance that with faith and hope in the risen Jesus we will achieve a more perfect life.

What I am saying, brothers and sisters, is this: flesh and blood cannot inherit the kingdom of God, nor does the perishable inherit the imperishable. Listen, I will tell you a mystery! . . . We will all be changed, in a moment, in the twinkling of an eye, at the last trumpet. For this perishable body must put on imperishability, and this mortal body must put on immortality.

(1 Corinthians 15:50–52, 53)

Psalm 38:1a, 2, 4, 5a, 6–11, 15, 17, 21–22

Father, I commend my spirit into your hands.

O LORD, . . . your arrows have sunk into me,
  and your hand has come down on me.

For my iniquities have gone over my head;
  they weigh like a burden
    too heavy for me.

My wounds grow foul and fester.
I am utterly bowed down and prostrate;
  all day long I go around mourning.
For my loins are filled with burning,
  and there is no soundness in my flesh.
I am utterly spent and crushed;
  I groan because of the tumult of my heart.

O Lord, all my longing is known to you;
  my sighing is not hidden from you.
My heart throbs, my strength fails me;
  as for the light of my eyes—
    it also has gone from me.

My friends and companions stand aloof
    from my affliction,
  and my neighbors stand far off.

But it is for you, O LORD, that I wait;
　　it is you, O LORD my God,
　　　who will answer.
For I am ready to fall,
　　and my pain is ever with me.
Do not forsake me, O LORD;
　　O my God, do not be far from me;
make haste to help me,
　　O Lord, my salvation.

Responsory

For those who want to save their life will
lose it, and those who lose their life for
my sake, and for the sake of the gospel,
will save it.

(Mark 8:35)

Prayer

Father, I feel that I am standing on the threshold between all that has been dear and familiar to me during this life and a new and fuller union with you in eternity.

My belief brings me joy and draws me to proclaim your goodness and mercy.

But I am afraid of making this next step, Lord, and the pain of my illness overwhelms me so that I feel abandoned.

Come to my aid with your grace so that in peace I may be a sign of hope to those I leave behind.

May your name be praised forever and ever!

Amen. Alleluia!

The Lord Is My Shepherd

Jesus comforts us with the promise
of his everlasting faithfulness.

My sheep hear my voice. I know them, and
they follow me. I give them eternal life, and
they will never perish. No one will snatch
them out of my hand. What my Father has
given me is greater than all else, and no one
can snatch it out of the Father's hand. The
Father and I are one.

(John 10:27–30)

Psalm 23

The LORD is my shepherd, I shall not want.
  He makes me lie down
    in the green pastures;
he leads me beside still waters;
  he restores my soul.
He leads me in right paths
  for his name's sake.

Even though I walk
    through the darkest valley,
  I fear no evil;
for you are with me;
  your rod and your staff—
  they comfort me.

You prepare a table before me
  in the presence of my enemies;
you anoint my head with oil;
  my cup overflows.

Surely goodness and mercy shall follow me
  all the days of my life,
and I shall dwell in the house of the LORD
  my whole life long.

Responsory

I am the gate. Whoever enters by me will be saved.

(John 10:9)

Prayer

Lord Jesus, I believe that having passed through the gate of life in baptism, I will always have your protection and comfort.

Yet today the pains of my illness threaten to overcome me and cause me to forget all the good things you have given me in this life.

I pray in confidence that you would send forth your Spirit to refresh and revive me as you have always done in the past.

May I continue to witness to your goodness in this life so that I may be with you at the heavenly banquet table in eternity.

Amen. Alleluia!

Father, I Seek Your Forgiveness

Turn to these prayers on those days when your physical illness brings about a sense of guilt for the times you have been selfish or hurtful. Perhaps you find yourself brooding about the missed opportunities you had to act as a Christian, or your spirit is heavy and you even begin to wonder whether your present illness is a result of God's anger.

The Lord wants you to unburden yourself of these anxieties. The Lord wants to remind you that the greatest measure of compassion comes only from the God who never stops loving you. You need to know that love in a personal way today. Seek the presence of God.

The Lord Listens

*Saint Paul urges us to free ourselves from the burden of sin
by submitting to the generous mercy of the Father.*

Do you not know that all of us who were baptized into Christ Jesus were baptized into his death? So that, just as Christ was raised from the dead by the glory of the Father, so we too might walk in newness of life.

Therefore, do not let sin exercise dominion in your mortal bodies, to make you obey their passions. But present yourselves to God as those who have been brought from death to life, and present your members to God as instruments of righteousness. For sin will have no dominion over you, since you are not under law but under grace.

(Romans 6:3, 4, 12–14)

Examination of Conscience

- Have I been allowing self-pity to overcome the sure promise of God's care for me?

- Have I cooperated with those who are trying to assist me in my illness and sincerely thanked them for their efforts?

- Have I let anger and frustration silence my thanksgiving for the blessings the Lord has given to me during my life?

- Have I been a sign of Christian faith and hope to those around me in the humble acceptance of my illness?

- Have I been persevering in prayer?

- Do I accept or seek to understand how my sufferings unite me to the death and resurrection of Jesus?

Psalm 116:1–8, 10–12, 17–19

Thanksgiving to a forgiving God

I love the LORD, because he has heard
   my voice and my supplications.
Because he inclined his ear to me,
   therefore I will call on him
     as long as I live.
The snares of death encompassed me;
   the pangs of Sheol laid hold on me;
   I suffered distress and anguish.

Then I called on the name of the LORD:
   "O LORD, I pray, save my life!"

Gracious is the LORD, and righteous;
   our God is merciful.
The LORD protects the simple;
   when I was brought low, he saved me.
Return, O my soul, to your rest,
   for the LORD has dealt bountifully
     with you.

For you have delivered my soul from death,
   my eyes from tears,
   my feet from stumbling.
I kept my faith, even when I said,
   "I am greatly afflicted";
I said in my consternation,
   "Everyone is a liar."

What shall I return to the LORD
    for all his bounty to me?
I will offer to you a thanksgiving sacrifice
    and call on the name of the LORD.
I will pay my vows to the LORD
    in the presence of all his people,
in the courts of the house of the LORD,
    in your midst, O Jerusalem.
Praise the LORD!

Responsory

Peace I leave with you; my peace I give to
you. I do not give to you as the world gives.
Do not let your hearts be troubled, and do
not let them be afraid.

(John 14:27)

Prayer

Father, you are ever faithful and patient, even when I have turned in upon myself during my illness.

I rejoice now because you have heard the sound of my voice and offered the life-giving comfort of your grace.

May I strive ever more faithfully to unite my entire self with your Son, who gave us an example of patient suffering, and may I be an example to others of the transforming effect of your forgiveness.

All praise and honor to you, source of life and mercy.

Amen. Alleluia!

The Lord Forgives

The call of Jesus never ceases even when we selfishly turn away.

Come to me, all you that are weary and are carrying heavy burdens, and I will give you rest. Take my yoke upon you, and learn from me; for I am gentle and humble in heart, and you will find rest for your souls. For my yoke is easy, and my burden is light.

(Matthew 11:28–30)

Psalm 32:1–7, 10–11

Lord, bring me relief from my guilt.

Happy are those whose transgression
   is forgiven,
 whose sin is covered.

Happy are those to whom the LORD
   imputes no iniquity,
 and in whose spirit there is no deceit.

While I kept silence, my body wasted away
 through my groaning all day long.
For day and night your hand
   was heavy upon me;
 my strength was dried up as by
   the heat of the summer.

Then I acknowledged my sin to you,
 and I did not hide my iniquity;
I said, "I will confess my transgressions
   to the LORD,"
 and you forgave the guilt of my sin.

Therefore let all who are faithful
   offer prayer to you;
at a time of distress, the rush
   of mighty waters
 shall not reach them.

You are a hiding place for me;
    you preserve me from trouble;
    you surround me with glad cries
        of deliverance.

Many are the torments of the wicked,
    but steadfast love surrounds those
        who trust in the LORD.
Be glad in the LORD and rejoice,
        O righteous,
    and shout for joy, all you upright in heart.

Responsory

Let anyone who is thirsty come to me, and let the one who believes in me drink. Out of the believer's heart shall flow rivers of living water.

(John 7:37, 38)

Prayer

Father, I know that you are forever faithful to those who believe and trust in you.

In my life I have tried to be a worthy follower of your Son, yet my own selfishness and weakness have often made me stray from his example.

As I near the end of this earthly life, I humbly ask your forgiveness of my sins.

Give me strength of mind and body so that I may continue to praise you by word and example for all the blessings you have given me.

All glory be to you, Father, together with your Son and the Spirit of your love, now and forever.

Amen. Alleluia!

Take Pity on Me

Jesus encourages his apostles and all of us who follow him to pray in faith to the Father.

Jesus answered them, "Have faith in God. Truly I tell you, if you say to this mountain, 'Be taken up and thrown into the sea,' and if you do not doubt in your heart, but believe that what you say will come to pass, it will be done for you. So I tell you, whatever you ask for in prayer, believe that you have received it, and it will be yours.

"Whenever you stand praying, forgive, if you have anything against anyone; so that your Father in heaven may also forgive you your trespasses."

(Mark 11:22–25)

Psalm 41:1–4, 7–8, 10a, 11

Father, grant me peace in your forgiveness.

Happy are those who consider the poor;
   the LORD delivers them
      in the day of trouble.
The LORD protects them
      and keeps them alive;
   they are called happy in the land.
   You do not give them up to the will
      of their enemies.
The LORD sustains them on their sickbed;
   in their illness you heal
      all their infirmities.

As for me, I said, "O LORD, be gracious
      to me;
   heal me, for I have sinned against you."

All who hate me whisper together
      about me;
   they imagine the worst for me.
They think that a deadly thing has fastened
      on me,
   that I will not rise again from where I lie.

But you, O LORD, be gracious to me,
   and raise me up.
By this I know that you are pleased with me;
   because my enemy has not triumphed
      over me.

Responsory

The sting of death is sin. But thanks be to God, who gives us the victory through our Lord Jesus Christ.

(1 Corinthians 15:56, 57)

Prayer

Father, I believe that you hear my cries and take pity on the anguish of my heart.

Extend your hand as I seek your loving pardon for the selfishness in my life, when I placed my own desires and comfort above others' needs and failed to offer you due thanks for your care and mercy.

May selfishness, my enemy, be overcome by your grace so that I may never cease to proclaim your praise now and in eternity.

Amen. Alleluia!

Have Mercy on Me

Jesus assures us of the unbounded love of the Father in the story of the prodigal son who humbly seeks mercy.

But while he was still far off, his father saw him and was filled with compassion; he ran and put his arms around him and kissed him. Then the son said to him, "Father, I have sinned against heaven and before you; I am no longer worthy to be called your son." But the father said to his slaves, "Quickly, bring out a robe—the best one— and put it on him; put a ring on his finger and sandals on his feet. And get the fatted calf and kill it, and let us eat and celebrate; for this son of mine was dead and is alive again; he was lost and is found!"

(Luke 15:20–24)

Psalm 51:1–4ab, 5–9, 12–15

Lord, you are good and forgiving.

Have mercy on me, O God,
   according to your steadfast love;
according to your abundant mercy
   blot out my transgressions.
Wash me thoroughly from my iniquity,
   and cleanse me from my sin.

For I know my transgressions,
   and my sin is ever before me.
Against you, you alone, have I sinned,
   and done what is evil in your sight.

You desire truth in the inward being;
   therefore teach me wisdom
      in my secret heart.
Purge me with hyssop, and I shall be clean;
   wash me, and I shall be whiter than snow.
Let me hear joy and gladness;
   let the bones that you have
      crushed rejoice.
Hide your face from my sins,
   and blot out all my iniquities.

Restore to me the joy of your salvation,
   and sustain in me a willing spirit.

Then I will teach transgressors your ways,
   and sinners will return to you.

Deliver me from bloodshed, O God,
  O God of my salvation,
  and my tongue will sing aloud
    of your deliverance.
O Lord, open my lips,
  and my mouth will declare your praise.

Responsory

We had to celebrate and rejoice, because
this brother of yours was dead and has come
to life; he was lost and has been found.

(Luke 15:32)

Prayer

Blessed are you, O ever-faithful and patient Father, for you never cease to accept me in my weakness.

In humility, I ask pardon for the times that I failed to respond as a follower of your Son and placed my own desires above all else.

Yet, while I have been looking only after myself, you have never ceased to love and care for me.

May my present illness purge me of selfishness and allow the inner warmth of your grace and peace to remind me of your loving kindness for the rest of my days.

Amen. Alleluia!

I Accept My Sufferings in Union with Jesus

These are times when you want to cast off the sufferings you experience. You wonder why you have to be incapacitated; you have so much to do and so many people who rely on you. You experience the discomfort of being dependent and you sometimes resent the caring hand others are extending to you.

Ask the Lord to enable you to understand and to make these words of Jesus your own, "Father, let it be done to me as you will!"

Hear My Prayer

*Our sufferings are not in vain,
as the writer of Hebrews reminds us.*

Endure trials for the sake of discipline. God is treating you as children; for what child is there whom a parent does not discipline? Moreover, we had human parents to discipline us, and we respected them. Should we not be even more willing to be subject to the Father of spirits and live? For they disciplined us for a short time as seemed best to them, but he disciplines us for our good, in order that we may share his holiness. Now, discipline always seems painful rather than pleasant at the time, but later it yields the peaceful fruit of righteousness to those who have been trained by it.

(Hebrews 12:7, 9–11)

Psalm 102:1–5, 16–20

God instructs us in our sufferings.

Hear my prayer, O LORD;
  let my cry come to you.
Do not hide your face from me
  in the day of my distress.
Incline your ear to me;
  answer me speedily in the day when I call.

For my days pass away like smoke,
  and my bones burn like a furnace.
My heart is stricken and withered like grass;
  I am too wasted to eat my bread.
Because of my loud groaning
  my bones cling to my skin.

For the LORD will build up Zion;
  he will appear in his glory.
He will regard the prayer of the destitute,
  and will not despise their prayer.

Let this be recorded for a generation
    to come,
  so that a people yet unborn may praise
    the LORD:
that he looked down from his holy height,
  from heaven the LORD looked
    at the earth,
to hear the groans of the prisoners,
  to set free those who were doomed to die.

Responsory

Unless a grain of wheat falls into the earth and dies, it remains just a single grain; but if it dies, it bears much fruit.

(John 12:24)

Prayer

Almighty God, I struggle daily to understand and accept your ways, which are not our ways.

While we seek comfort and pleasure in this passing life, you remind us that suffering will be a part of our journey to eternal life with you.

Please help me to bear with my own sufferings more patiently so that I will not be distracted from the call and example of Jesus who, through his suffering came to reign with you for all eternity.

Amen. Alleluia!

You Are Forever Faithful

Jesus assures us that we are constantly under the care and protection of the Father.

Therefore I tell you, do not worry about your life, what you will eat, or about your body, what you will wear. For life is more than food, and the body more than clothing. Consider the ravens: they neither sow nor reap, they have neither storehouse nor barn, and yet God feeds them. Of how much more value are you than the birds! And can any of you by worrying add a single hour to your span of life?

(Luke 12:22–25)

Psalm 8:1–6, 9

The Father's care is everlasting.

O LORD, our Sovereign,
　　how majestic is your name
　　　　in all the earth!

You have set your glory above the heavens.
　　Out of the mouths of babes and infants
you have founded a bulwark
　　　　because of your foes,
　　to silence the enemy and the avenger.

When I look at your heavens, the work of
　　　　your fingers,
　　the moon and the stars that you have
　　　　established;
what are human beings that you
　　are mindful of them,
　　　　mortals that you care for them?

You have made them a little lower
　　　　than God,
　　and crowned them with glory and honor.
You have given them dominion
　　　　over the works of your hands;
　　you have put all things under their feet.

O LORD, our Sovereign,
　　how majestic is your name
　　　　in all the earth!

Responsory

If you then, who are evil, know how to give good gifts to your children, how much more will the heavenly Father give the Holy Spirit to those who ask him!

(Luke 11:13)

Prayer

Father, sometimes I feel alone in my illness and I am afraid of the future that seems so dark and uncertain.

I know that you are always with me, although I must continue to knock down the wall of self-sufficiency that surrounds me.

Help me to feel the warmth and see the beauty of your loving presence in creation so that I may always give thanks for your care and receive strength of mind and body to accept the trial of my illness.

May your name be blessed today and always, for you are forever faithful.

Amen. Alleluia!

God Highly Exalted Him

Saint Paul reminds us that Jesus' great humility led to his suffering and our salvation.

Christ Jesus,
who, though he was in the form of God,
did not regard equality with God
as something to be exploited,
but emptied himself,
    taking the form of a slave,
    being born in human likeness.
And being found in human form,
    he humbled himself
    and became obedient to the point
        of death—
    even death on a cross.

Therefore God highly exalted him
   and gave him the name
   that is above every name,
   so that at the name of Jesus
   every knee should bend
   in heaven and on earth
      and under the earth,
   and every tongue should confess
   that Jesus Christ is Lord,
   to the glory of God the Father.

(Philippians 2:5b, 6–11)

Psalm 131

Jesus, refuge of the humble

O LORD, my heart is not lifted up,
   my eyes are not raised too high;
I do not occupy myself with things
   too great and too marvelous for me.
But I have calmed and quieted my soul,
   like a weaned child with its mother;
   my soul is like the weaned child
      that is with me.
O Israel, hope in the LORD
   from this time on and forevermore.

Responsory

Blessed are the poor in spirit, for theirs is the kingdom of heaven.

(*Matthew 5:3*)

Prayer

Praised be you, O Christ, for your kindness and fidelity and the humble acceptance of suffering for our salvation.

Through the strength of your loving Spirit, help me to shoulder any infirmities and be at peace in the knowledge that in union with your death on the cross I may also participate in the glories of the Resurrection for all eternity.

Amen. Alleluia!

I Put My Trust in You

*In the face of his own painful suffering and death,
Jesus offers words of consolation.*

I tell you, my friends, do not fear those who
kill the body, and after that can do nothing
more. But I will warn you whom to fear: fear
him who, after he has killed, has authority
to cast into hell. And I tell you, everyone
who acknowledges me before others, the
Son of Man also will acknowledge before
the angels of God.

(Luke 12:4–5, 8)

Psalm 31:1–2, 9–10, 14–16, 19

Trust in God as a father.

In you, O LORD, I seek refuge;
　　do not let me ever be put to shame;
　　in your righteousness deliver me.
Incline your ear to me;
　　rescue me speedily,
Be a rock of refuge for me,
　　a strong fortress to save me.

Be gracious to me, O LORD,
　　　for I am in distress;
　　my eye wastes away from grief,
　　my soul and body also.
For my life is spent with sorrow,
　　and my years with sighing;
my strength fails because of my misery,
　　and my bones waste away.

But I trust in you, O LORD;
　　I say, "You are my God."
My times are in your hand;
　　deliver me from the hand of my enemies
　　　and persecutors.

Let your face shine upon your servant;
　　save me in your steadfast love.

O how abundant is your goodness
　　that you have laid up for those
　　　who fear you,

and accomplished for those
who take refuge in you,
in the sight of everyone!

Responsory

The Mighty One has done great things for me, and holy is his name.

His mercy is for those who fear him
from generation to generation.

(Luke 1:49–50)

Prayer

Father, even while my body is weakening, may my spirit continue to find its strength in you.

I trust that you will always be near to me to lead me through whatever trials bodily sickness may bring.

May I continue to witness to the Resurrection promise of eternal life and thus bring a sense of faith and hope to those around me.

May your name be blessed today and always.

Amen. Alleluia!

My God, My God

Saint Paul encourages us to be unique examples to all.

We also boast in our sufferings, knowing that suffering produces endurance, and endurance produces character, and character produces hope, and hope does not disappoint us, because God's love has been poured into our hearts through the Holy Spirit that has been given to us.

(Romans 5:3–5)

Psalm 22:1–2, 9–11, 14–15, 19, 22–24

United with the suffering of Christ

My God, my God,
   why have you forsaken me?
   Why are you so far from helping me,
      from the words of my groaning?
O my God, I cry by day,
   but you do not answer;
   and by night, but find no rest.

Yet it was you who took me from the womb;
   you kept me safe on my mother's breast.
On you I was cast from my birth,
   and since my mother bore me
      you have been my God.
Do not be far from me,
   for trouble is near
   and there is no one to help.

I am poured out like water,
   and all my bones are out of joint;
my heart is like wax;
   it is melted within my breast;
my mouth is dried up like a potsherd,
   and my tongue sticks to my jaws;
   you lay me in the dust of death.

But you, O LORD, do not be far away!
O my help, come quickly to my aid!

I will tell of your name to my brothers
and sisters;
in the midst of the congregation
I will praise you:

You who fear the LORD, praise him!
All you offspring of Jacob, glorify him;
stand in awe of him, all you offspring
of Israel!
For he did not despise or abhor
the affliction of the afflicted;
he did not hide his face from me,
but heard when I cried to him.

Responsory

If any want to become my followers, let
them deny themselves and take up their
cross and follow me.

(Mark 8:34)

Prayer

Lord Jesus, your words on the cross give me strength and hope.

I do not ask to be relieved of my sufferings but to be helped to accept them, trusting in the will of the Father and the hope of securing salvation for all.

Help me to persevere in confidence when pain brings the darkness of despair so that I may live in the glory of the resurrection in union with you, your Father, and the Spirit of your love.

Amen. Alleluia!

My God, Rescue Me

Jesus warns his followers to remain strong.

Then they will hand you over to be tortured and will put you to death, and you will be hated by all nations because of my name . . . And many false prophets will arise and lead many astray. And because of the increase of lawlessness, the love of many will grow cold. But anyone who endures to the end will be saved.

(Matthew 24:9, 11–13)

Psalm 71:4–5, 8a, 12, 17–18

Growing old in Christ

Rescue me, O my God, from the hand
    of the wicked,
  from the grasp of the unjust and cruel.
For you, O Lord, are my hope,
  my trust, O LORD, from my youth.

My mouth is filled with your praise,
  and with your glory all day long.

O God, do not be far from me;
  O my God, make haste to help me!

O God, from my youth you have taught me,
  and I still proclaim your wondrous deeds.
So even to old age and gray hairs,
  O God, do not forsake me,
until I proclaim your might
  to all the generations to come.

Responsory

If you sow to the Spirit, you will reap eternal
life from the Spirit.

(Galatians 6:8)

Prayer

Father, as the span of my life grows shorter, complacency as an enemy leads me to take for granted your goodness in the promise of salvation for your faithful.

Through the inspiration of your Spirit help me to praise you continually for the people and events that have entered my life.

Help me to stand firm to the end in the face of any difficulties I might encounter in union with the sufferings of your Son, Jesus.

Amen. Alleluia!

I Pray for Those Who Suffer

You realize today how much your illness turns you in upon yourself—how much your self-pity simply adds to the feelings of depression and powerlessness. You begin to think that you are the only person who experiences so much fear, frustration, and inconvenience, and this creates a burden of loneliness.

You know in your heart that there are others, known and unknown to you, whose sufferings are more burdensome. Reach out to them in prayer and know that you are doing a caring deed from the confinement of your sickbed. Commend them and yourself to the care of a loving God and thus lift your lonely burden from your shoulders.

My Soul Is Thirsting

Saint Paul reminds us that in our baptism we have already died with Christ so that we might live in glory with him forever.

So if you have been raised with Christ, seek the things that are above, where Christ is, seated at the right hand of God. Set your minds on things that are above, not on things that are on earth, for you have died, and your life is hidden with Christ in God. When Christ who is your life is revealed, then you also will be revealed with him in glory.

(Colossians 3:1–4)

Psalm 63:1–8

Father, may I be worthy of the kingdom.

O God, you are my God, I seek you,
    my soul thirsts for you;
my flesh faints for you,
    as in a dry and weary land
        where there is no water.
So I have looked upon you in the sanctuary,
    beholding your power and glory.
Because your steadfast love
        is better than life,
    my lips will praise you.
So I will bless you as long as I live;
    I will lift up my hands
        and call on your name.
My soul is satisfied as with a rich feast,
    and my mouth praises you with joyful lips
when I think of you on my bed,
    and meditate on you
        in the watches of the night;
for you have been my help,
    and in the shadow of your wings
        I sing for joy.
My soul clings to you;
    your right hand upholds me.

Responsory

Strive first for the kingdom of God . . . and all these things will be given to you as well.

(Matthew 6:33)

Prayer

Father, mere words cannot express the inner peace that Christian hope in eternal life has brought to me.

Yet, I have also felt the fear and uncertainty that weighs upon us in illness when the familiar and comfortable in our lives is taken from our grasp.

I pray now in hope that those who have died from illness may have merited your promise of eternal life with the risen Jesus.

Give me the strength to continue to bear patiently my sufferings on behalf of those to whom illness has brought despair, so that one day we may praise your name unceasingly in eternity.

Amen. Alleluia!

I Pray for Those Whom God Has Called to the Other Side of Life

Today your body's weakness is a frightening reminder of how frail your life is. You realize that in spite of all the remedies of medicine, your body will not live forever. You are reminded of friends and loved ones who have gone to the other side of life. They share the fullness of comfort and joy that you seek as well.

Place yourself in union with those who know eternal life and the full meaning of Jesus' resurrection. Thus, you can know that the Lord never abandons his loved ones. God cares for us in life and in death.

Age After Age

We pray for the dead with confidence that they have been shown mercy and given everlasting union with the Father.

Then one of the leaders of the synagogue named Jairus came and, when he saw Jesus, fell at his feet and begged him repeatedly, "My little daughter is at the point of death. Come and lay your hands on her, so that she may be made well, and live." So he went with him.

And a large crowd followed him and pressed in on him. While he was still speaking, some people came from the leader's house to say, "Your daughter is dead. Why trouble the teacher any further?" But overhearing what they said, Jesus said to the leader of the synagogue, "Do not fear, only believe."

(Mark 5:22–24, 35–36)

Psalm 90:1–3, 9, 12, 14

Jesus—refuge in life and death

Lord, you have been our dwelling place
    in all generations.
Before the mountains were brought forth,
    or ever you had formed the earth
      and the world,
    from everlasting to everlasting
      you are God.

You turn us back to dust,
    and say, "Turn back, you mortals."

For all our days pass away under your wrath;
    our years come to an end like a sigh.

So teach us to count our days
    that we may gain a wise heart.
Satisfy us in the morning
      with your steadfast love,
    so that we may rejoice and be glad
      all our days.

Responsory

Now he is God not of the dead, but of the
living; for to him all of them are alive.

(Luke 20:38)

Prayer

Father, your Word among us brings us life.

Remember those who have made me a better person by entering my life.

As you raised the daughter of Jairus to life, so, too, have mercy on the departed.

Give me the grace to grow in hope that my own sufferings may bring growth in faith and union with you in eternity.

Amen. Alleluia!

Alleluia Forever!

Saint Paul exhorts us to be examples of hope when other people despair in the face of the finality of death.

But we do not want you to be uninformed, brothers and sisters, about those who have died, so that you may not grieve as others do who have no hope. For since we believe that Jesus died and rose again, even so, through Jesus, God will bring with him those who have died. Therefore encourage one another with these words.

(1 Thessalonians 4:13–14, 18)

Psalm 146:1–7, 10

People of hope will sing praise to God forever.

Praise the LORD!
Praise the LORD, O my soul!
I will praise the LORD as long as I live;
    I will sing praises to my God
      all my life long.

Do not put your trust in princes,
    in mortals, in whom there is no help.
When their breath departs,
      they return to the earth;
    on that very day their plans perish.

Happy are those whose help is the God
      of Jacob,
    whose hope is in the LORD their God,
who made heaven and earth,
    the sea, and all that is in them;
who keeps faith for ever;
    who executes justice for the oppressed;
    who gives food to the hungry.

The LORD will reign for ever,
    your God, O Zion, for all generations.
Praise the LORD!

Responsory

For as all die in Adam, so all will be made alive in Christ.

(1 Corinthians 15:22)

Prayer

Lord Jesus, you accepted your death, and with confidence in the Father and love for all people you proclaimed, "It is finished."

May all the good that your servant has done during life merit eternal peace, so that this faithful servant may rejoice in your presence together with the Father and the Spirit of your love.

Grant that those of us who remain to carry out your mission of love and life on earth may have the same confidence and peace as we cross over into the eternal kingdom.

Amen. Alleluia!

Praise Is Yours!

As Jesus nears the end of his earthly life he prays for the eternal welfare of his followers.

Father, I desire that those also, whom you have given me, may be with me where I am, to see my glory, which you have given me because you loved me before the foundation of the world.

Righteous Father, the world does not know you, but I know you; and these know that you have sent me. I made your name known to them, and I will make it known, so that the love with which you have loved me may be in them, and I in them.

(John 17:24–26)

Psalm 65:1–5, 8

Not an end, but the beginning of eternal life

Praise is due to you,
  O God, in Zion;
and to you shall vows be performed,
  O you who answer prayer!
To you all flesh shall come.
When deeds of iniquity overwhelm us,
  you forgive our transgressions.
Happy are those whom you choose
    and bring near
  to live in your courts.
We shall be satisfied with the goodness
    of your house,
  your holy temple.

By awesome deeds you answer us
    with deliverance,
  O God of our salvation;
you are the hope of all the ends of the earth
  and of the farthest seas.

Those who live at earth's farthest bounds
    are awed by your signs;
you make the gateways of the morning
    and the evening shout for joy.

Responsory

And I heard a loud voice from the throne
    saying,
"See, the home of God is among mortals.
He will dwell with them;
they will be his peoples,
and God himself will be with them;
he will wipe every tear from their eyes.
Death will be no more;
mourning and crying and pain
    will be no more."

(Revelation 21:3–4)

Prayer

Blessed are you, Father, for you lift us out of the finality of this world to experience unending peace and joy in union with you.

For those like me suffering from illness, I pray that we may have confidence in your unending care.

For those whose illness has brought them to the end of their lives, may they experience your mercy and be found worthy of eternal citizenship in the New Jerusalem.

Amen. Alleluia!

I Thank God for My Recovery

Today you feel a deep satisfaction and gratitude for restored health. You don't want to forget that the Lord listened to you in the frustrations and fear you voiced in illness, that God sent people to bring comfort to you and nourished you with reassuring words of presence and love. You want to be able to look back at the time of your illness as one in which you grew in trust of God and in the love God manifested through those who cared for you.

You want to see this time as one that brought new insight into responsibilities that you can take up anew with energy and faithfulness. You realize that the illness you have borne can make you more understanding of those who enter your life in the future burdened by illness.

I Bless Your Name

We are called to give thanks to the Lord for the good we have received lest we forget that God is the source of all things.

On the way to Jerusalem Jesus was going through the region between Samaria and Galilee. As he entered a village, ten lepers approached him. Keeping their distance, they called out, saying, "Jesus, Master, have mercy on us!" When he saw them, he said to them, "Go and show yourselves to the priests." And as they went, they were made clean. Then one of them, when he saw that he was healed, turned back, praising God with a loud voice. He prostrated himself at Jesus' feet and thanked him. And he was a Samaritan. Then Jesus asked, "Were not ten made clean? But the other nine, where are they? Was none of them found to return and give praise to God except this foreigner?" Then he said to him, "Get up and go on your way; your faith has made you well."

(Luke 17:11–19)

Psalm 145:1, 8–9, 13c–14, 17–18, 21

God has heard my cries for help, Alleluia!

I will extol you, my God and King,
　　and bless your name for ever and ever.

The LORD is gracious and merciful,
　　slow to anger and abounding
　　　　in steadfast love.
The LORD is good to all,
　　and his compassion is over all
　　　　that he has made.

The LORD is faithful in all his words,
　　and gracious in all his deeds.
The LORD upholds all who are falling,
　　and raises up all who are bowed down.
The LORD is just in all his ways,
　　and kind in all his doings.
The LORD is near to all who call on him,
　　to all who call on him in truth.

My mouth will speak the praise of the LORD,
　　and all flesh will bless his holy name
　　　　forever and ever.

Responsory

Be merciful, just as your Father is merciful.
. . . for the measure you give will be the
measure you get back.

(Luke 6:36, 38)

Prayer

All praise and honor to you, Father,
for the strength of mind and body
that has been restored to me.

May this experience of restored life
lead me to praise your name more
faithfully for the rest of my days.

I humbly ask for the help of your
Spirit, for the light and courage
to be a more faithful follower of Jesus,
especially in being a source of
comfort and healing to others who
are in need.

Amen. Alleluia!

The Eucharist:
The Lord Gives Me
the Gift of Himself

In your illness, you are especially
sensitive to people reaching out to you
in love. Most particularly, Jesus extends
a loving hand to you today through the
Eucharist. He comes to visit you in your
sickbed as a friend. He wants to give
you strength to combat your weariness.

Look to the Lord to hold you in his love
because he knows the demands of
suffering and the care of a loving
Father.

I Give Thanks

In giving the gift of the Eucharist,
Jesus bestows on us the promise of life .

Jesus said to them, "I am the bread of life. Whoever comes to me will never be hungry, and whoever believes in me will never be thirsty. But I said to you that you have seen me and yet do not believe. Everything that the Father gives me will come to me, and anyone who comes to me I will never drive away; for I have come down from heaven, not to do my own will, but the will of him who sent me. And this is the will of him who sent me, that I should lose nothing of all that he has given me, but raise it up on the last day. This is indeed the will of my Father, that all who see the Son and believe in him may have eternal life; and I will raise them up on the last day."

(John 6:35–40)

Psalm 111:1bc, 3, 5, 7–8

Thanksgiving for the gift of life

I will give thanks to the LORD with my
    whole heart,
    in the company of the upright,
      in the congregation.

Full of honor and majesty is his work,
    and his righteousness endures for ever.

He provides food for those who fear him;
    he is ever mindful of his covenant.

The works of his hands are faithful and just;
    all his precepts are trustworthy.

They are established for ever and ever,
    to be performed with faithfulness
      and uprightness.

Responsory

On the last day of the festival, the great day,
while Jesus was standing there, he cried out,
"Let anyone who is thirsty come to me, and
let the one who believes in me drink."

(John 7:37–38a)

Prayer

Jesus, you understand our weakness and give us the very source of all goodness and strength in the gift of your body and blood.

Just as my body craves food to sustain life, so, too, my spirit is thirsting for you as illness overwhelms me.

May this Communion, your gift of self, bring joy and comfort to me in the face of pain.

All glory and honor to you.

Amen. Alleluia!

The Sacrament of the Anointing of the Sick: The Church Comforts Me

Today you have received the special ministry of the Church through the sacrament of the anointing of the sick. Open yourself in thanksgiving to God, who has turned this time of your illness into a source of special grace for you.

Through the prayers and the anointing that you received, be open to the assurance of special spiritual strength in the days ahead.

You Increased My Strength

*Paul assures us that with the promise of the Lord's assistance
we are never abandoned in the face of sickness and death.*

When this perishable body puts on
imperishability, and this mortal body puts
on immortality, then the saying that is
written will be fulfilled:

"Death has been swallowed up in victory."
"Where, O death, is your victory?
   Where, O death, is your sting?"

The sting of death is sin, and the power of
sin is the law. But thanks be to God, who
gives us the victory through our Lord Jesus
Christ.

Therefore, my beloved, be steadfast, immovable, always excelling in the work of the Lord, because you know that in the Lord your labor is not in vain.

(1 Corinthians 15:54–58)

Psalm 138:1–2b, 3, 6–8b
God is ever faithful.

I give you thanks, O LORD,
    with my whole heart;
before the gods I sing your praise;
I bow down toward your holy temple
    and give thanks to your name for your
        steadfast love and your faithfulness.
On the day I called, you answered me,
    you increased my strength of soul.

For though the LORD is high,
    he regards the lowly;
    but the haughty he perceives
        from far away.

Though I walk in the midst of trouble,
    you preserve me against the wrath
        of my enemies;
you stretch out your hand,
    and your right hand delivers me.

The LORD will fulfill his purpose for me;
    your steadfast love, O LORD,
    endures for ever.

Responsory

The prayer of faith will save the sick, and the Lord will raise them up; and anyone who has committed sins will be forgiven.

(James 5:15)

Prayer

Lord, I know that you never abandon us, even when we place our needs and sufferings as obstacles to your abiding presence and care.

I thank you for the strength I have received from the anointing of your Church.

May this sacrament give me renewed strength and the healing power of your grace so that I may live the remainder of my life in closer union with you.

I pray this in union with your Son, who always showed compassion and bestowed healing on the sick.

Amen. Alleluia!